Library Inspector

or The One Book Library

Library Inspector

or The One Book Library

David Hart

Nine
Arches
Press

The Library Inspector or The One Book Library

David Hart

ISBN: 978-0-9931201-3-8

First published August 2015 by:

Nine Arches Press
PO Box 6269
Rugby
CV21 9NL
United Kingdom

www.ninearchespress.com

Printed in Britain by:
The Russell Press Ltd.

CONTENTS

This book is dedicated to my grandson
Daniel Hartworth
and to my grandaughter
Raina Klaces

INTRODUCTION

During 2012 into 2013 I was Library of Birmingham Poet, which is to say before that new library in Centenary Square opened. My appointment came from an insider suggestion, not from a thought I had had previously, nor from an advertised commission. I was not paid and had no fixed plan. My formal appointment was circulated internally online.

The Central Library was still in use then, the new library was being built. For various reasons being the 'LoB Poet' (as my formal badge said) did not work out well and I resigned before the new library was opened. The intention had been for me to be the poet of the transition, a challenge I had relished, and this I was, into the period of the pre-opening. No period of time had been specified. I engaged as best I could for a year or more and got to know many of the community libraries better. As I write this, the Central Library is soon to be destroyed.

Also now, 'the biggest public library in Europe' has come up against Birmingham City Council cuts (passing on cuts in Government allocation), and will lose almost half its opening hours and most of its professional staff. At the last hour, professional Archives staff survived this absurdity. What reputation in Europe does the City Council have now and with what consequences for the city's own population?.

My starting point for what has become this book was specific. One day, when the outer shell of the Library of Birmingham was built, I was in Centenary Square and I had this thought, this experience rather:

> The new library is very big
> and we are very small.

Out of this developed a fantasy of tiny libraries, starting from the One Book Library, in a notional area of mid-Wales, where I was born and where I lived my young life. Neither the geography nor the placing of the fantasy libraries now resemble in much detail that real place. I have re-invented it.

The sequence developed as fragments and has only relatively recently taken on the continuity it has now. There was, back in 2012-13, no notion of an Inspector, I drifted later into involving him.

Whatever it was at any one time I imagined I was doing, the list in retrospect does follow through what might be called the real-surreal. From time spent on Holyhead Mountain and then on Bardsey Island, Enlli, came *Crag Inspector* (Five Seasons Press, 2002), *The Titanic Café closes its doors....* – demolition in the Bristol Road (Nine Arches Press, 2009), and most recently *Misky*, happenings in Worcester (Flarestack Poets, 2011). I am 75 now, which seems surreal in itself. Most of my life has been spent in Birmingham, about as far from the sea in Britain as it is possible to be.

David Hart
February 2015

There is a monk far out at the sea's edge, I think it is a monk, the tide far out, yes, it is dawn, the beach of flat sand, he must be a monk, facing the sea, very still, a good half mile away but must be, yes, very still, at least half a mile, the water a flat seaway, the sand and the sea on the same level to the horizon, hard to tell where the sand ends and the sea begins. He stands there, the monk, must be, very still himself, sand, sea and monk still, in black he is, wholly still, doesn't turn, doesn't walk back.

From my Inspector's rent-free hut, in post now
I am ready, not ready precisely but give it a go.
The hut is half a mile inland, today's tough schedule
will take me across the river, then seawards and up
Old Crow Hill on to the coastal cliff path and a few
yards further up to the

      Six Book Library shack on the slant

and I find it SHUT, no
         gloss, no exegesis by note
         in the window 'sorry'
such as 'Gone for a long walk, sorry', or 'Try again three
months from now,' apology, or 'Had enough of this lark,
you try'. And no scent of toast either, no apple
         on the chair outside.

It doesn't surprise me one day she'd be gone.
All three of the card holders I've known these
         several years now
           come Whit
said so, I knew June in the city, must have moved

back again, gone, I suppose to the city, said
at every opportunity she needed to
manage fifteen books minimum, and the
previous, Mervyn, wanted Kilimanjaro at best, at least
Snowdon in his log book, spoke of manning a
balloon library. Shall I wait? Hoped for a mug of
tea on such a day, an egg sandwich at best,
                    and chat.

Down the cliff path now to the

Three Book Library Boat

rising from the waves at Blue Sands Bay.
I see it anchored in the small harbour for what
seems a long moment hanging in the air

until the Three Book Library Boat
does a magnificent pirouette
hitting the harbour wall,
the heaped lobster pots as well,
the Three Book Library Boat
high and dry, beached and open.

I dive in.
O lovely Three Book Library!
No books, though: a slip of paper on the table
is blown into the air and I catch it, it says,

ALL BOOKS OUT ON LOAN TO
      Mr GRIMSHAW WHO IS
      SWIMMING FOR HIS DEAR LIFE
BOOKS ALOFT
      AND NO HOPE HONESTLY

signed,
Three Book Boat Librarian, at long lunch,
back maybe.
Now along the sea-level path past the
next quay
and the 'Pig & Mackerel' as was, closed now.
I tramp the beach and by way of the causeway
quick now I ask my old legs, *booster, bester*, joyously,
let's say, across the sparkling pebbles and to the

Four Book

on Mog Island.
CLOSED FOR STOCK TAKING,
I knock at the closed shutters, I sing very loudly
Abide with me
all the parts, I try to kick the door in
and it breaks my ankle almost.

More than enough for one day, I trek back –
left my bike last week at the
Ten Book on
Bryn Mawr,
walked it down there, what was I thinking? And left it
in trust to the valley.
No use a bike round here anyway, no roads for a car
neither.
Up early tomorrow
and over one of the wooden bridges
across the Werry these days only
a trickle,
up the steep rough land to
Glob Hill and here I am at the

Ten Book Library

is very busy today, perhaps twenty-eight of us,
we queue on the hill below this shed on stilts.

We are dizzy with expectation, we are shivery
with doubt, a record attendance according to the
archived records (I have done my homework
but have in the queue no precedence, I am
                    humbled).

The thing is, free chocolate word has it has been
promised. All around, look, mist as far as can be
seen. Now up the hill come six more, all
out of breath, one as he arrives panting is
                    close to tears.

The door above the ladder squeaks open,
            the librarian squints at us
            from this angelic height,
                sighs, pauses, sighs,
stands proud, wets her finger and holds it high,
                    'Mmm.'
She smiles, if it is a smile,   making sure everyone
    gets a look at her large new spectacles.
She calls out into the mist, 'The books
            are being serviced, you will
                understand   it's a fine
                tradition at this   time of year, less salt
                in the wind,   less wind,
                believe me,   leave
            your names, and what I do now,
            as the old hands will know, I
                    draw up a list
of appointments, OK? and I'll let you know
            by postcard,   consequent upon
            the reinstating   of the postal service.'

I wave,
it's me I'm here professionally, you know me, I have
a smart badge.   The door closes.

               The next morning we are all
where we were in our places in the queue, frozen,
               some dead even,
               a nightmare.

Am taking the day off to sleep. I wake mid-afternoon
in my grace and favour hut to a vision, I am
sitting with toast and coffee out the back on a wicker seat
with a view across the stream – in April a river –
only it's not St Michael's Mound but an ocean-going liner
with the church on it, hundreds waving from the
several decks, in high spirits singing, 'Hey ho, hey ho!'

A man in a red suit leaps off the ship, comes
running loopily and
               tells me,

     'The next great library,' –
      it's a voice from Orbiter Twinkle 42 –
     'will be a mushroom planted
      on one of the moons of Jupiter,
      books will be needed there –
      so a few diehards have it –
      but miniscule, to be read
      through microscopic lenses.
      There will be a drinks machine.
      and a mirror. The whole of the
           world's archive
      will be stored in a blouse button,
      a shirt stitch will secure the whole mind

of a tortoise, poetry will be stored
in a budgie's beak, the whole
music library in a plastic rib.
Thought is being given as a gambit
to staff grades and how to
        grow coffee.'

I'm away now over the stream
around the ancient Mound of Indices and

at the river crossing an encounter with
Elwyn Emmanuel and his donkey Tom,
floppy bags of books, if books, slung over
him restless. Elwyn says, deep voiced,
    'Did you by any lucky chance
    see the great tappet vulture above
    the quarry this very morning, I ask you?'
Expecting something of the kind I say,
    'Was I still in bed or having a think over
    intense porridge?' I promise to catch up
with him again near Quarry Hill, near the busy

Eleven Book

this week or next. 'You're all talk,' he says, 'head full
    of commas, semi-colons. Now then them
    vultures I've been telling you, –'
I was patting old Tom's rolling head. 'In the bags,'
I said, 'how many books?' 'Three' he said, 'heading to
the **Six Book** then the **Four**, the **Six** after that and
then – well you make it up as you go along, you lead
and I follows. No pay rise neither, not that I've heard
        from the fiction called
        Headquarters.'

Thus it is books get returned to their proper base,
return a book anywhere round here and
Elwyn will on his daily round
rehabilitate it when he takes time off from
watching vultures
that no-one he tells sees nor ever
believes exist here, perhaps he means
the series *Thomas the Vulture Gets His Man*, the whole
illustrated series.

So we part and I walk and I stumble and I walk
and I look to the sky and I stumble and I walk
and I arrive in high professional spirits at the

One Book Library

in the bluebell wood in a shack hospitable, I imagine,
to passers-by, the one book available for loan
for a whole year. And if the book is out, the yearner
is welcome here for an apology and bluebell tea, may
relish a natter with Mr Garvey who offers also a game
of greased chess and wins always, is allowed to know
what's good for you, if you want your drink,
and when there are no bluebells there is dried leaf tea
and
to business, the loan years passing, for the one book –
The Poetics of Loss –
will fracture or go soggy, in equal measure maybe,
will make no sense to those who have not memorised it,
he tells me again wistfully, it will be left on the step to be
taken for 10p,
which will mark the end of the one-book library. Today
it is out in the name of Gladys Merilee
with a smudged return date.

Onwards, and in the morrow's mist and around the
great bog, I sense I am required at Bog Moor, the

Two Book

which is a library with one chair. Widow Halfpenny,
old hand at negotiated librarianship, has extrasensory
anticipation. Someone, she tells me, very soon now
will knock at the door three times, and
   here he is, One Legged Clem, crying inside elastically
as he hands Widow Halfpenny
            Saint Grotius on Silent Doubt,
out of a frayed bag, wool of a goat. 'I pray you', bowing,
he says, 'forgive the delay, I had hoped it would be
            a mere seven years, you do
remember me, I see you do, fifteen now, and my
silent doubt not much mitigated, and not, in truth
I confess, the book's fault. Is *Scones in a Day* available,
that fine old baking book, has old Grump Jones
returned it? No? Thirteen years.'
            And leaves.
Widow Halfpenny smiles, glows even, as she re-shelves
            Saint Grotius.

It has been good to witness a transaction, on now
through the glow of dandelions to nearby Shad Lane
and a library that has from the first confused me,
I find the atmospherics at the

Five Book

to be sentimental blister-splitter, gavotte-clot,
Dorothea, never quite in tune with herself.
As I enter she spies me and begins her welcome:

'Head, fingers, knees and toes,
toes and knees,
knees, toesies, head and one finger, two finger flip
and thumb through our five books
with care, see. Please.'

She awaits my applause. The scribble on the wall
of this one room cottage says,

THE BOOKS
Love in a mist,
Love in a bog,
Love on the beach,
Love with fresh cakes,
Love by the fire
and to dream here.

Now here comes the readership, the elderly woman
on roller skates, having raced no doubt along Shad Lane
like tin cans rolling, and without a word takes
all the books out and will, as I hear said,
a week later bring them all back and she will skate
all the way home – I go out and watch – she is
smiling always, so Dorothea tells me. She tends now
the tray of Meadow Mushrooms. She recites
close into my left ear

'I shall retire in office on full pay,
that athlete of books, Dorothea,
I have given her the key,
awake or asleep
she will no longer bother me,
I shall take my leave with a good conscience
early.'

Sighing my way away, I decide to lay low as I pass after
a mile and three quarters the hazardous
Library of Visions
and negating my inclination to steal away home I reach
with some relief the

One Book

and I can't remember if I ever know if Mr Garvey
is staff or user – did I say 'user'? Do I mean 'customer'?
'Reader'? Qualified staff, unqualified, a temp, or
a passer-by doing it for expenses: a sandwich and tea?

It says here in red ink, ACT TWO,

If anyone wishes to borrow this one book
if it is not out on loan already and if no-one is on duty

they may leave a promissory note to say
why they need it and by what date they intend

to return it. The librarian is every day busy
somewhere or other in his innerly life rife
with expectation, and if one week or month

there appear here in good order a walker or two
or a group of five
they will be given a great speech of apology and

couch grass tea, conversation being mandatory, this
is a draft renaissance.

Mr Garvey is blind now, recalls my voice. He leans
against where a shelf would be, I ask professionally

if *The Poetics of Loss* is in stock or out on loan currently.
He hesitates, he coughs, he says he doesn't know really.

I say he could retire, he cries heavy tears, I say I'm sorry,
I say how wise and necessary his library with one book simply.

Back to my hut by way of getting lost in the wood,
no melioration of bluebells now, no happenstance
                of precipitous bliss nor
allocation of Angelic Host butties, I am in the middle
                dark, I feel my way
from tree to tree to gate to hut to door, I light a bold
        candle, I find my notebook and pen: Doom

        wants to enter my room tonight
                for my education,
                        as if all the stars have gone out
and the moon has spun wildly into
                        another galaxy, I must
        rehearse my know-how
                before continuing my timetabled
rounds: but for now and for ever I am
                in the dungeon of my island hut
        without books,
                without wine,
        in a dungeon without prisoners, am myself
        a prisoner without a dungeon, in my heart
                no roses, see here
a crypt deeper than the dungeon and not
        without bones and there is
                too much light.
I collide with the skeleton of a stag
  set into a wall and trying to die,
and for a moment this seems the whole

conflagration of my soul, I am unable
to find the steps. *Bring me a mince pie
and some fresh ground coffee.*
    A magpie is on the roof,
wants my eyes and my shoelaces
        in that order.

I trained in nights and days, is this truly
an old, a very old, or a fresh new day?
Is it into night or out of it? Must get *far* out
        riding a book
and freshly vacant.
        So,
resting on a whim in the wartime bunker
    across the river on the side
        of Bryn Glass Bore Da
on my way to the

Library on Wheels
        stuck
    these years I was told in best mud I see

someone has left a book on the chair, open.
A thin, flexy man peers in, asks if he can
        join me, eases
  his way in, sees the book, pauses, sits
  well away from it.
        I touch it and it flaps open.
The man nods his head at this, solemnly.
Scribbled on the open pages, 'Look,' I say,

   'We are made of viable stuff, perhaps.'

The man points under the chair
where I see now an empty cheese sandwich carton

and a crunched beer can, and a handkerchief.

The man leaves, I want to read more of the book
    but must move on to inspect the
        Door to Door

its eloquence via the farms and cottages these
virile months now curtailed wholly, staunched

in mud on the slant deep in. I have my pen and my
Renaissance Motifs record book enabling me
        on the steps to
sit and write. But before I can settle, what's this?
I pull out from under the up-slant of the
        Door to Door
        this notice,

'I write, dear book geezers, that where what will be
        will be
    we aim on course to serve willy-nilly
    ere we can shift and move and halt
        to serve again
          hey!'

and I shall interpret this according to regulations, here
where it goes on, look,

    'Please note that a pale woman in mourning
        bleak-eyed
    will be rushing to grab the pulse of the
    essential mind-thing in a lovely fake gold
        quire.'

Did I note this today? It is not my birthday.

As I walk past I see she is scrawling words
        across the words printed there.
Hers, I'm sure, will be dark words. She will
        look up, as the note says,
'she will ask for a red pen, which I shall give her.
She will sketch a bright sun over her own writing.
She will look up at me and smile. And again smile.
She will say, 'It's a lovely day, we both know that.'
She will leap up and away, leaving the book at
                your feet
        open where the sun strikes.'

But here, as if to rescue me, comes
                Emlyn Emmanuel, always
an interruption, always an
                obliqueness, always welcome, and
Tom, patient donkey. 'Mud,' I say.
    'Mud indeed,' says Emlyn, lowering himself on to
an oak stump, 'what's up with Job Jenks? Picked his
strawberries yet, written his novel yet? Needs pills
or a good woman.'
    'What? Who?'
    'Jenks up at Bryn Glob, the **Ten Shed**. Scar tissue.'
    'Have you seen this?', I say, handing him the note
from under the carcass of the **Door to Door**.
    'Invisible writing? Par for the course,' handing it back.
    'But look, *She will say*, and the rest.'
    'Sermon to the bibs and bobs under the stones, earwigs
and the gulls' ribs and the snot, I told you.'
    'No, Emlyn, surely not.'
    He's away now, up and with a 'Come along, Tom'
they've gone.

My report interrupted, I scribble that I have heard
neither snores nor tears, nor books out loud

from inside the **Door to Door**, neither lament
nor laughter, leave it. On now to
stomp my way up the side of Cromlech Fawr
to the cliff path and find there, as surely there is,

The Man on the Bench

looking out to sea, his head shaking.
He holds a bag tight under his arm,
should I give him a notice, make a sound
as of speech? Is he a man aglow,
does he sleep rough on bench or beach
or in a hideaway where dreams...? I say,
'Mind if I sit here, been walking all night', I lie,
forgiveably surely, 'lovely bleak morning,' I say,
          'been doing a tough job.'
He says nothing, prepares properly nothing to say
          and I move away.

So it's down the cliff path past the first quay, past
the harbour and on and on, a woman seems to be waving
from Stitch Cottage, I wave back, and here I am now
at the
Twenty One Book

at the tideline, SHUT, and I wait, wait and I wait,
not for anything or anyone, only that to wait
          seems right,
I wonder what *right* might be, dear friends
and professionals reading this, got it sad, waiting.

I am opening my mind now to where I can see
three women dancing barefoot on the sand, one
     the librarian and one

the local MP and another
the policewoman
for this whole area. Library
                SHUT FOR MERRY, I sit
                and watch and

mother said, do not cry until there is time for it
and place apart, steady your teeth in dry bread,

make it easy for yourself, she said, make it hard.

Playfully, I sling my best book for a joke,
        like a broken song,
defenceless now on this good rock
against claws and nightmares,
against stark whims and inmost fires
catastrophic. It sinks into weed,
into cleft, into the darkest chide
of stinging things and claws freed
from human laws, from
                mindlock. One waves
and now another and now the third, all
beckoning.

I turn and cut across inland, route-marching myself
until up the shale by sundown to the

Fourteen Book

on Glad Top, the old farm tool shed renovated, O my
absurd timing, but she's here the new librarian, Kerry,
beautiful, settling in well, she says, very keen, engagingly
knowledgeable, great news, says just closing, apologises,
lovely eyes, would I mind returning tomorrow? Will
have the kettle on. Next day

has been abandoned. I walk smartly in now through
the open door and begin to act my heart out as if to
restore the art and the magnetism, the educational
facility, the head snoozing on the best read there
ever was.

Sober now. One shelf, no books: I lie, a book called
Fish for Smart Cats
is open at – too sad to say – and I find the following,
in a neat wild hand, nicely on a torn-off side of a
sugar box:

    – A.Huxley: Descriptive Catalogue) ... *he actually <u>saw</u> 'those
    wonderful originals in the Sacred Scriptures the Cherubim.*
    – L.Wittgenstein: *In fact, in this form the expression will
    be constant and everything else variable.*
    – V.Woolf: *accumulating, welling up moment by moment,
    runs like quicksilver a dozen ways at once.*
    – I.Murdoch: *'I mean I shall do what I want to do.'*
    A.E.Housman: *XXVI The half-moon westers low, my love,/
And the wind brings up the rain;/ And wide apart lie we,*
    – Virgil (tr.Royds): *Goes forth to greet the sun, and stands aghast.*

'Job done, have fun. Kerry, I shall return.'

Keep moving, bind now the mind and heart to legs and plan,
cross-country again, evading by an alert margin the

Library of Brief Visions

(too much, man, too much) and
    skirting the locked St Michael's on the Mound
beside the river, get a fix on the

29

Door to Door 2, which is a

motorbike and opuscula-pocketed side car,
toppled half
into a reed bed. Nice bright
painted sign on its visible side,

WE ARE THE WISH TO PLEASE
BECAUSE OF THE SEA BREEZE
LIBRARY

I sigh, as is appropriate for a functionary in my position,
I bring out a pen and the record book to sit and write.
I see and pull out from the side car in sludge this
photocopy, one of perhaps twenty:

'There is an ever open door for dancing,
for dancing on mud, we that are blessed with mud,
never need ask what for our life here,
only dance now on mud,
so stuck in mud we pause and think,
thus thought enlivens and confuses us, we will
reach you somehow with a book
if you need us,
we can come to you through mud
if you will welcome us,
we won't promise a whole van
to reach you but we do
have a book or two.'

I find in the sidecar pocket one book: a revised
Saint Grotius on Silent Doubt, Volume ii: Shout
It.

Another day, another stretch of the imagination
where neither Kathleen and Trudy, nor Isabel
and Anne seem anywhere hereabouts, neither
Sidecar nor Van
in any kind of operation any time soon. Where is
Elwyn Emanuel and Tom the donkey? I need
at this roaming hour Elwyn's negation of duty, his
dismantling of affirmation. Where next?

I have overheard from a conversation as I was passing
Rising Farm on my way to the Sacred Hill rumbling
that there is a woman walks north then
south all evening, this way that way, across
Barnacle Bay at sunset
known locally as 'Dreamland'
aka the low tide Putting Green, holding open Goethe's
Theory of Colour
to the moon and yet eyes glazed
near the
Missing Book Library.
I am on my way there. How simple it would seem
to stop her and ask,
but how to decipher even my own notes
so as to know what to ask, and wisely?
Even to know in myself *how* to be there.

And
I have dropped my report cards
O weeks ago
copied from my notebook or as Report Direct,
burned the notebooks, O such broods
of notes they littered the floor of my hut and
to complete the job I welcomed the wind in,
'Be my guest, do your worst.'
Don't tell.

Must get over to Mogg Island anyhow, will do it
tomorrow after a dream or two, Mogg
is home to the **Four Book**, meanwhile
              here I am
in what was once the

Library in Entropy

where I find *Classic Images of Great Escapes* lying
                   open
on the marble floor. If a librarian is here, as alive
                   as air,
I wish they would show themselves, give me
                   a fair
chance at True Inspection: interview, day book
        and so on. No-one about, move on,
              for it is my job
to inspect the Old Books inside St Michael's
on the Mound by the stream that in April
becomes a river. I am here now. But hey,
              look,
in the churchyard a man of some critical age
              is sat on a grave
with on a pile of books, 'Metrical psalms', he tells me,
'for constipation', he's a poet (I asked), tells me
              his vocation is to be
'a submariner of stories, a wasp, a gnat, a grot,
a grappling looper of language who slips and slides
 to become in God's good time an acceptable cog
   in the divine wheel'. I ask does he hear psalms
as he sits and reads, do they become a cacophany, do they
        uprise stark through his whole throat?'
              He smiles, shyly.
Now of a sudden he has upped and gone leaving
the books atumbling.

I bow to where he was and to the
scattered books. My notebook opens in my pocket,
it flaps about and closes. A young woman passing
pauses and stares at me, grins and walks on.

I find myself after walking in a contrapuntal whizz
towards the

Library of Visions, Rock Point,

near Barnacle Bay. Inside I begin to say
to her back whatever it was I might have thought –
'Nothing quite fits,' she says, 'with anything else,
at the same time everything fits together
gleefully – but not by God – nothing
can be studied, everything must be.' Only now she
sees me. I introduce myself, 'Okay for an inspection?'

She turns her head this way, that way, says, 'Would you
like a bath with me in the sea? We may find we can
share a deep story? The News, would you agree,
is too newsy
and never newsy enough? We are news now, you
and me in an as yet
un-newsy sort of way. Truly do you
like cornflakes only in even numbers? I do, please stay
for breakfast.'
I reply, 'Clouds will now form an orderly queue.'
She says, 'Waves, too.'
'I am here to inspect – I cannot know my place
until I can inspect your records.'
'Might you love me?'

All very well, I tell myself on my way dishevelled
and not in a straight line all along the coast
missing out the
Lighthouse Library of Journals
to the

Torn Brochures Library

a tent at the tip of Devil's Quay across the estuary
from The Scud trackway, has a banner flapping
from a high pole:

ALL FLYERS, FACT SHEETS, CARDS AND
BROCHURES, ARE BEING FREED NOW
THIS MORNING FROM THIS 1876 PRIZE-
WINNING TENT LIBRARY, SENT OUT INTO
THE GRACIOUS BREEZE LIKE UNTRAINED
PIGEONS. THEY FLY, ARE FLOWN – HAS MY
VOICE CHANGED? – BY THE OBLIGING BREEZE.
BLESSED BE BREEZE!

O more than a breeze now and the wild sea is
having a whoopy frolic of fun with this billiously blowy
library,
no sight of Jimmy Smith-Edwards, a devout
and conscientious librarian these many years.
I watch a Camp Sites brochure fly then drown, a box
of what I know to be Holy Sites is in the air
doing somersaults. Those bobbings and chirrups
flapping in the sea are not birds, not birds.

Needed a camera for this, no camera, let it be for bright
rumour to tell it.
On now but not for long: 'Hey there,
Inspector!' It's Elwyn,

trailing tired Tom, I call back,
'How's business?'
'Having a wander, us'. They have come alongside.
I ask, 'On the way from where to where?'
'Not the right question.'
'Ask it yourself, then.'
'Did I tell you there was this Turkey Vulture?'
He watches my eyes. He says, 'High above the bog it was,
high, high, twice now. Hadn't stolen a book but
king of the skies, *my* eyes are attuned, isn't that
right Tom?' The donkey nods his head.
I say, 'You're sure of that?'
'You calling me a liar, Inspector, Sir?'
'I've seen a black-headed gull,' I say, 'before breakfast.'
He says, *'The Sore Throat of the Last Shaman* is missing
from the Three Book, nicked, I
have nicked it.'

Write up the encounter later, now
keep walking, past Mogg Island, the causeway
invisible at high tide, past Splat Crag now, thank
the holy angels no library there. Past
Crab Island, thank a drunk surveyor no library there,
past the **Three Book**, let not the fate of Mr Grimshaw
fret my professional heart, and on the hill, look,
the stranger pleased always to see me,

The Man on the bench

where I sit now, I am patient, he is staring far out
                        from far in,
I want to say the splat of sea is splattting The Splat,
dousing the rock of ages, I say nothing. His bag is
slung over his shoulder as if soon to journey.

From his centuries of experience, can he advise me?
I ask nothing. He sniffs.
I speak, I say I am modest with words. He sniffs again.
The sun on its turn towards the horizon seems
so to blend bloody with the greying blue of the sky –
said *the heavens* almost! One day not so
far hence there may come a moment when all
blemish of word will be smoothed out, but to
extinction. He sniffs, thought-reader. I wake
and he's gone. I kick a white stone, it
   rolls away.
   I jump up and kick it again
   and again
   all the way home.

Days pass, I have had visions of missing pages
and now on a professional itch this thin day I must
make a return visit to the

Two Book

and it seems smaller. The Widow Halfpenny
has gone, I see, someone has scratched into the table,

  Much missled (sick).

I asign myself to this table as a quasi-professional sit-in.
There is a knock at the door, I guess who it is,
he staggers in, he says, 'Who the fuck are you?'

I volunteer the chair, he waves it away, he sniffs,
we are into the little rite of time passing.
He sways standing as if about to sing, speaks
slowly, slowly, sacredly, into my eyes he says,

'I see on the shelf
Saint Grotius on Silent Doubt,
I beg you to let me
re-borrow it.'
He opens his goat's wool bag, I reach for the book,
I place it carefully in the bag, he gestures
to the signing-out book, eyes me, asking if he
should make this transaction formal, for the record.
I am about to say, 'There is a second volume,'
but I have left it in my hut's loo. He would be right
not to believe me. I wave him away.
He wants his dirty look to last. He leaves.
He returns, says, 'How many years this time the loan?'
He becomes the size of a matchstick man
                    and is gone.

Must risk the Sacred Hill this morning, I am sick.
Now, outside the curtained cave on the said Hill –
high above the

Library of Visions

visible also from my hut's rear pippin tree – I queue
                    in wind and rain
                    for a rare opening,
or so word on the piss had it. I have here
no authority, here merely extramurally, on my own
dire account. Whatever happens now and now
                    and now
          will happen in mist.

          Form a queue, this must be
a devious other place, my writ from the Big Bang
may not run here, I form

a queue of one. Perhaps
if I sigh enough and pause and sigh again.
Nothing. No-one
in front of me and no-one following. But a door opens,
a book is hurled out, the door closes. The book opens,
a blank is fired, misses, sharps me, it is best now if I

cut my gains and losses and visit Widow Bell at the fine
Old Vicarage
not on St Michael's mound but beside it, next the river,
and she lets me in, starts talking:

'The brain cell by cell is beautiful,' she says, –
in her study shelved around with books aplenty, makes me
drowsy, 'and here,' she says, pouring from the white pot,
'your *lot*,' no pouring for herself, offers no tight
cherry loaf, no crow-shit cake, no chocolump. 'The brain
animates – drink up! – must choose mind minor keys
with which to play sonata-like – tea adequate? –
to play awry to learn.' I am staring. She says,
'Go away and
with better timing
return with a neater line
in drollery. Keep off
my books.'

Time now – after a couple of days off asleep laughing
or drinking tea in dreams and eating toast and expecting
elves to visit – must chance it to

Lighthouse Journals, Library of,

where I become along its corridors as I'd feared
a crab crawling, drying out along the headland filled

with private want, asking who will ache with me.
But this truly is me in this the library, little me, picking
at indices, running my finger down a page
and down another until – The librarian, Frank App,
is staring at me, has caught me
humming, I remind him who I am and he says,

'Set an example then,' I look around me
to indicate, *An example to whom?* He shakes his head
and says, 'Everything is in good order, I like my job.'
'You mean *Frog Spawn News,*
           Baking with Poisonous Mushrooms,
           Industrial Scale Aphorisms,
           Sea Bed Poetry,
           Kindness to – '
'All in order,' he says, 'and the rest. I expect very soon
a pay rise and more holidays. Do you want cocoa?'

I was claustrophobilised. Out now in the fresh air I pull
a woolly hat out of my bag,
           I pull it down over my ears and
after a few yards on concrete towards land wish I'd
           accepted the cocoa and perhaps a biscuit,
chocolate even,
           and reflect as best I can on my brief life
as a crab.

The day seems properly back on course now I am
inland towards the

Library on Stilts into Clouds

waiting with Caroline the Third for a delivery
           of books made from feathers

when I encounter a sad man stumbling about in the
very bog itself attempting, as I come to understand,
the sale of cast-off school editions of Shakespeare from
a library God knows where, in some upstart city, pages
scribbled on or missing, given him for free, he says,
he'd been a student of DIY, had played endemically
Bertram and Malvolio with mates and the king whom
one doesn't name. I buy one book with some wild garlic
and he cries aloud like – I imagine – a ghost would or a
cockerel, or deeply religious empty falling
shelves.
    I have to see graves now,
        I had forgotten graves,
            I walk from bog to wood back to
            bay to cliff to bog to hills
                to lowland to those familiars at the mound,
                roll down it to the river
                    where I throw a Mother of Pearl
                    across a whole lay of the buried
                    and wish.

Here's a kiosk I know well, gulls a waggle,
a note hangs on the closed shutters to say
what the shutters say brutally: SHUT.

No gloss, no exegesis, no *Sorry*, such as
Gone for a long walk, sorry, or *Try again three
months from now, sorry* or *Had enough of this lark,
you try, sorry.*
            No toast, no tea.

On the beach behind it, a book, pages blowing,
a page detaches and flaps into me,

As the astronomers tell us that it is probable that there are in
the universe innumerable solar systems besides ours, to each
of which myriads of utterly unknown and unseen stars belong,
so it is certain that every man, however obscure, however far
removed from the general recognition, is one of a group of men
impressible for good, and impressible for evil, and that it is
in the eternal nature of things that he cannot really improve
himself without in some degree improving other men.

The Kiosk opens: 'Hey you!' I smell tea and toast,
gulls arrive ahead of me, from the kiosk a smile,
I don't resist, I begin to recite *As the astronomers tell us*.
                    I am high
                    on pretence
                    and lost.

Notes kept and not kept. One day I recall I did visit

The Sky Trail Library

which you won't see if you are not there in mist
at Scar Rock, some two miles north of the Bog.
Ein Tad did not call me, duty did. Never has been
staffed, this phantasm. I pretended access down
to the books kept in a secret place in the UR-stock.
I fingered in air these words: *synapse, impulse, cells,*
transmission, I run my fingers over *neuron, cell,*
honeycombe, chamber, and look here: *auricle, ventricle,*
arena, lobby, corridor, pad, wondered if out there
in the wastes I could apply them, for a regrading.

Now in my hut this night
I touch with my left hand my own right arm,
I touch with my right hand my left ear,

my left knee now, touch my genitals, my navel,
touch my eyes, over each eye a finger, rush of blood
to my head, into thought. Let me
                              run now
and call and
fall and
          slow down you idiot, not a place to die.

So it was dawn by the time I had crossed right over
south west to the hill, to the Bench, notes made
          en route and
afterwards and lost mostly on scraps and anyway
this reminisce today on the way to

The Man on the Bench

He is hugging the bag to himself.
When I sit he says, 'I've been here centuries,'
so I say, 'No, you haven't,'
          'Yes, I have,'
          'No, you haven't,'
          'Yes, I have,'
so I say, 'How long then, how many centuries?'
          'What does it matter, you won't believe me.'
          'What's in the bag?'
          'A holy relic.'
          'You mean a dog's leg.'
This has shut him up.
          'Do you recall this?' I say, pointing
at the incoming tide far below us, shining,
and the fishing boat, 'Does this
          wash right over you?
He stares far out, to the horizon or higher, thereabouts.
I pull out of my pocket a bunch of slips of paper,

I read from one at random, I say,
'The books burn.'

Back down the hill inland to my hut, plenty to
occupy me
without resolution, piles of books
on the floor mostly
to inspect at night, though I doubt
anyone will believe I work at this job
through hard-won experience, gifted to me
after patient lazing, enviable, my innocence
until destroyed by books
splendidly.
      I am taking
the inland route this morning
around the goats
and along Hwyl Lane on to The Scud to the

Brochures Library

where I find the Broch Librarian swaying
      at the end of the quay
pleased at what she has chucked away,
      claiming a grip now
with both sore hands
      on the flag pole bending
towards her,
      and calls out.

I confess a haze of time
      without enumeration
passing as if marked
      NOT TO BE LIVED IN.
There have, I believe,

been more library visitations
or at the very least visitational
            good intentions that might
better be sung, and
            did she drown, has there been
a funeral? Must ask
            and note it.

Here is a book washed clean by the sea,
taken and cleaned out and thrown back
at the Barnacle Bay slipway. It is in a language
far from my own or from hereabouts, here
on the rocks at Drone Cove another, and one
   being reported by a man who signals
            from the far rocks.
So there occurs a shelf vacancy at Scatt Crag,
O exquisite tideline

Twenty-One Book Library

and at the Causeway the rowing boat launched
and sunk. The book saved, look, photos of
Jesus at the well, of a Circus high walker too, and
over the page, of Barnacle Bay a memoir. Here
            a sketch
of myself asleep in my hut rising on the dew,
            and here
a man waving the large brain
            of a feather pen.

So with gladness now at last to the

Three Book

on the coast and not far from my hut, only to find
this note waving from the door locked shut:

OUR SHORTER OXFORD FOUND
WASHED UP NEAR SPLAT CRAG
YOU WILL ALL BE PLEASED TO KNOW
ALTHOUGH WET ALL THROUGH
LIKE PUDDING
NO SIGN OF MR GRIMSHAW, THE
LIBRARY IN MOURNING UNTIL
FURTHER NOTICE. TRY THE
SIX BOOK
POSSIBLY

So from the last phone box along this coast
I think it my duty to ring the Divisional Director
whose answerphone says he is on holiday
in the Arctic, standard message, no date
for his return, and the phone hanging dead, so I
        buy some cheap postcards
at the ferry terminal and send them library class
to all branches:

> *Best to continue to date-stamp, to date stamp,*
> *to the end of next year, to the end date stamp,*
> *until the future   is clearer.*

Hurried then over to Bog Moor trusting a hunch,
noted when I got there:

A man is tearing pages slowly and carefully
out of a large notebook at the edge of the bog
as I walk past. Wish I could record the scribble
as each page hovers
on the breeze. He turns and smirks and
rips more, lets them fly.
                    I say, 'You are the man

who paced up and down
outside the Tea Shack these many years past.'
'I'm winning,' he says, 'piss off!'

I stay. He waits. I stay.
            He waits. I smile. He turns
back to the deep bog and hurls the rest of the book
as far as it will go. It makes a splash like an eagle
                    landing
                upside down.

He walks away, he pauses, he comes back, he says
                    nothing.

I walked away, I went back, we stood facing each other,
we shook hands, we parted frightened at what we had
                done like actors
                scar-faced.

Days pass, it says here. On my way now up from
            my hut to the

Tea Shack Six Book

where when was there tea ever? It says
        SHUT. But the door
can be swung open.
No evidence of recent use, but since I was here last
there is now
                on the floor
a pile of books and another and another, someone
        has been playing book towers.

I search for a written record of transactions: nothing.
Tea? No tea. Coffee? No coffee. Chocolate? No

high cocoa hard, no chocolate dripping. Librarian?
  Nothing in the ABSENT book,
    and no stray note.

Ah, but someone is mouthing a skype, which can be
transpostnatalunpetrified on screen as

'Your library speaks volumes,
      ha!
I was a borrower here once,
you had grey eyes and a deft wit,
that year of blessings, I was smitten,
    real smitt, did't you know
        that?'

I hear Tom the donkey approaching, his hefty breathing,
lungs not what they were, and here is the ever drifty
Elwyn Emmanuel at my shoulder, he points at a book
on the sad table. 'Came in and eyed the title page of that
weeks ago, Inspector, Sir, only then it was being slept on
by the cat, *Theories of Authorship* by Tredgold, John, editor,
by right it belongs on the bench up the cliff there, surely.
What d'you reckon, let it rot here or what?'
  I ask, 'Is anyone in post here, are you clued in to that?'
  'Does it matter? Don't *you* know, Inspector?'
  'There's a confusing turnover.'
  'Absence, you mean, Inspector.'
  'Everything's under control, everything's fine.'
  'Did you spot the Hooded Vultures, Inspector, a pair,
over the Bay yesterday? My heart went into ineffably sweet
convulsions, truly ineffable, big words for big times, drank
two pots of tea at the Rose Point caff and six extra-sugar
doughnuts, Tom ate five. We stumbled away then, both
dizzy. You're not
interested.'

I thanked him – and Tom too – for kindness.

Emergency: **Librarian in pyjamas**

A man in pyjamas and frippery
               is rushing towards the wild sea
at Barnacle Bay waving
               hopelessly to nobody.
I want this man's rushing and waving
               utterly alone
to be worth something.
               I get closer, at the foamy edge,
he is up to his neck shouting,
               'My book, my book,'
and when I am up to *my* waist
               in waves he shouts,
'Blunder, foolish, holy gooly bad mistake,
               it was a MIS-MIS-MISTAKE!'
And evaporates.

Back up the hill to the shed that is consecrated the

Ten Book

again closed and bustling
               the queue of the dead outside wait.
I arrive in bright sunshine, I prod the dead, they fall.

I ask the dead why they are here, why they were here.
'Don't know,' in a chorus of mutter, 'don't know, habit,
must have been habit, must have been love, leave us.'
I prompt them by whispering,
               'Plot, suspense, love.' Nothing.

The hill now is covered in concrete for the first

DIY plastic houses.

I slide down the formica track,
the library door knows me, it squeaks open, the librarian
appears, waves,
sighs, pauses, sighs, waves,
standing proud, wets her finger and holds it high,
says 'Mmm.'
I remember, I remember, Miss Thomas. (Don't mind me). She
smiles at the dead
and through me.

There is a down and an up track. Last track of the day
now to the

Fourteen Book

where I find all fourteen on a table outside
in the wind, where a notice says

WEDNESDAYS AND SUNDAYS

I calculate by how weary I am that today is Friday:

PLEASE BROWSE
AND ANYONE WITH A TICKET
OR WITH HONEST TICKET INTENT
MAY BORROW –
WHEN NOT OUT ON LOAN –
FROM THE CATEGORIES LISTED:

BLAZE ROMANCE x3
SENSUAL ROMANCE x2

HISTORICAL ROMANCE x1
SCIENCE FICTION ROMANCE x1
FANTASY ROMANCE x 1
HORROR x2
JANE AUSTEN x1
MEMORIES OF WAR x1
COMIC VERSE ANTHOLOGY x1
PHOTOGRAPHY FOR AMATEURS x1

When next I find a library with a librarian in post
and in the flesh present
I shall endeavour to remember to ask where I can find
a doctor. A private thing, heat, nightmares, missing
the lights of the city, expecting a helicopter. Meanwhile
I have arrived at

The Bench on the Hill

He is here, sitting legs stretched out, hands open.
I sit, I say, as if wearing the very best suit
I shall buy one day, 'Would you like this
very afternoon to collaborate on a great scheme
to investigate the deep meaning of poetry *per se*?'

He spits far away over the cliff, it returns wet,
could have won him a medal. I don't say this.
I do say, on impulse, 'What's in the bag? I say,
'Curious that you have your feet on it, so what's
                    the secret?'
He sniffs.
I,
I threaten to report him for vagrancy 'this very day'.

He sits more passively than ever, barring conversation.
We sit in noiselessness a long time. I say, 'Help me?

Please?'

He gets up and walks on higher. So I, too, set out
but skippity-hop down the cliff steps to Drone Cove
where I see a man I recognise as the

Fourteen Book's
vagrant librarian
pissing against the sea wall and singing *Jubilate*.

I imagine I am further out across the rock pools
telling myself
I am due free time, the tide wheedling out
further yet. The man's
Jubilate is bouncing off the cliffs. Now he is away
up the spiral steps
rolling his head to *Jubilate* until he and the sound
have gone. Out at sea
a quarter of a mile away a man is waving urgently
from a dingy
that he knows me. I wave in return and again wave
but can do nothing
only wonder at his departing what jokes are lost.

Now on my way home by a detour, late afternoon,
a man is rising up out of the river near the church
on the mound. He is trying to speak, surely he is trying
to share something deeply long hid. His lips open and
close, his face is a rag. He sinks back into what again now
is still water.

I write myself a note in bed late:

Your job is libraries
sub-section Books
sub-section Journals

sub-section Other
sub-section Librarian welfare
no sub-section Rock pools.

Next day, down at the coast, a bream is lying
on the stone jetty at Devil's Quay
                    looking up at me.
I ask what it's like far, far out at sea.
The bream tells me it's a better place to be
than lying here on the hot quay, *be a friend to me*,
its mouth open, its gills snappy this-that way.
I ask if it will sing to me, I am asking nicely.
It says, *Only if you will swim far out with me.*
'I am unable to swim far out with you,' I say.
Throw me in alone then, wave goodbye to me.
'You must sing to me first, then be on your way.'
I sing, I sing, I sing only far out in the deep sea.
And says, eyes wide, *Are you going to kill me now,*
what does the poem say?
I wait and wait, I watch the bream die. I say
sorry.

Drawn after these heavy work days by a hunch
up the Sacred Hill,
I overhear this to and fro, don't know
where from, no moving lips, no word-clat-clat
I can see, my eyes are closed
that's why, and I hear waves, I hear,

  'The waves insist, dictate first
  and last, without mind or blood.'
  'But what's the time, Mister?'
  'What time is that, lad?'
  'Time to understand, Mister.'

'Play the glow-worm, lad, the waves
fear that, day or night, fear it.'
'You're just making that up, Mister.'
'I am, lad, I am.'

They have gone.
I have to see the graves again,
down Inner Being hill to the graves,
I had forgotten what it is to stand by graves,
I remembered, I forgot again,
I throw a stone
across a whole crowd of gone,
across the blackberries and past the yew
into the river.

My job is books, the books is job,
must get up the cliff path again to

The Man on the Bench

He has no bags now,
I look behind the bench and under it and behind it.
He says, 'Bastard!'
When I sit down he says, 'I knew Judas Iscariot.'
　　'You are a fabicator, a memory miscreant.'
　　'He was picked on.'
　　'The hard cash tempted him.'
　　'Someone had to do it or there'd have been no –'
　　'Go on.'
　　'*Poet!*'
　　'No bags now.'
　　'Books burn easy.'
　　He says, 'Stranger.' He gets to his feet, bends down
and picks a daisy and gives it to me. I hesitate. Crying

I receive it.
                He's gone.
The bench creaks and splits and collapses. So it's

back to the churchyard, see if the dead are ready
to be trained as librarians, at the very least to
borrow books, to chat, to wander in and be met whole
or at least in part. Or collectively for us all
                to fake it.

I wake at midnight,
who was it, the dull heap under the blanket
  on the cart along the lane behind my hut?
        Someone I know? I hope not,
  pulled past my hut by the lame, stumbling donkey,
            look, sad, sad,
        led by men uniformed, masked
            and speechless.
    Each midnight now as I wake and
            walk out,
    someone or someone else every night
        under the blanket
at the turn of the track as I watch and wait
        under a full moon
  a body it must be under a blanket pulled in all
    weathers on the ratchet of a cart
        at a steady pace, blanket loose,
  on a body if it is a body, I believe I see a shoe
        and a loose hand –
        Is that lump a head? –
        pulled by the lame donkey,
        must I write this?
        Must I *read* it?

At last a call after days, weeks, arrives
on the west wind to the

Twenty-One Book, it may be

rumour only, one day I see it,
the next I don't. Word on the wind
has a *Breeches Bible* in pages unconfined
and a *Dialect of Dreamland* muddled.
These may be wild, wild whispers, of the
      twenty-one books
I have heard said fifty titles, more,
a hundred and seventy, I lie. I wish.
It is rumoured Mrs Roberts of her own

Old Manse Library

up the track from here has closed her curtains
      and lives by candlelight.
I have seen flickers. I put a note a while back
through her door, *I have a copy of the Black Book.*
      I lied. But like a bat in light.

Not far up the track early morning to the

The Man on the Collapsed Bench

A book has been left where habitually I sit,
the seat laid now on stones piled up flat.
There is no *Take me* note. Is the book here
by oversight, or is it here to frighten me? Is someone
nearby now watching me? Anyway,
it is a book, at last a book if wantonly. It's a manual
on surgery, well-thumbed, corners smudged and

turned down. As I roll the pages there are scribbles
in margins:

Forget this when nervous.
We are made of viable stuff. Really? Hurts.

I have not picked it up, only flicked through.
Here's another scribble,

If I attempt this, they will stare at my eyes.

I am afraid, the book unrestrained here worries me.

Leaving the bench and the cliff track downhill
inland across-ways and up again on to the
rough Dead Snail Lane between the Sacred Hill and
Glad Rag Top I find the

Twelve Book Tea Shack Library

in shade
REALLY SHUT.
No kisses,   no eclectic verse,
no *Sorry*, no message
such as *Gone for a long run in the long run, sorry,* or
Try again three years from now if it helps, sorry or
Nightmares, sorry.

No scent of best toast either.

It doesn't surprise me one day she'd be gone,
all three people I've known in the queue these
several years come Whit
thought so, said so, 'O the Tea Shack Library!'

we'd sigh,
in love really. Eleri, gone now
I suppose to the allegory for which she longed. Shall I
wait? Don't want to leave, hoped at the very least for a
mug of tea and a glad eye.

Have I mistaken **TWELVE** for **TEN** or for
FOURTEEN or for any library open still and busy
with herself, Eleri, awake anticipatory?

Be content instead with the ragged walk, with
getting from somewhere to somewhere else listed
as OPEN once
upon a good time and a time it was
pleasing and whatnot, arrived out of good breath
and

waking from a dream roller-skating the quay
and off the edge into the grey sea, can't face
trekking back across the hills now to the

Ten Book on Bryn Glass Wait,

but decide to
stay hut-home instead and I swear now that
as I approach my hut from mind-inside a body
under a blanket is being taken out. I call, 'Wait!'

Forget it. Wearily at dusk carrying a slice of toast
as if it will save my life
and a tin mug of tea I do climb the hill to the

Ten Book

where the notice on this door tells me:

WORD HAS IT THE BREAK-IN
WAS CO-ORDINATED. ANYONE
FOUND PLAYING A MOUTH ORGAN
IN A DREAMY SORT OF WAY,
WILL BE PROSECUTED

What break-in? What mouth organ? Enough.
I return to my hut and write from memory:

Approaching again

I have come across fields, winding through valleys,
I have come over hills and through bog carelessly,

canu is in my ears and its progenitor *y môr*,
daft ideas arise for telling –
look what's in my bag here, Mother of Pearl
and seaweed
and sound, bag full of sound, waves breaking
against my heart, the tide
goes out and the tide is out and the tide *is* out
and it is right to write,

'Dear One Book Librarian:
Do you have the book that is a pebble with one eye?'

I am glad to wake to find I have not sent this. But send it.

During the next night a red kite comes in vulture-sized
and drunk on blood
and is never sated, claws into my neck, dew flutters me
attempting rescue, a voice, *Dream cariad, dream*
beyond dream
to escape dream,

and in the landlocked hut
the tide –
      Disguised as a monk now I set out
past the **One**, past the **Library of Visions**, past **Two**
at the bog, avoid **FIVE** at Shad Lane and crawl,
believe me crawl, up the fifty-two steps, I am at
Top Crag now at the

Nine Book

where I find a well-scripted large print notice nailed
to the locked door:

DEAR COLLEAGUES, BORROWERS AND
YOU NOSING AROUND FOR A FREEBIE TEA
YOU SO-CALLED COLLEAGUES ESPECIALLY
      YOU INSPECTOR
    WILL UNDERSTAND WHY
  LEAVING THE OFFICE TABLE SET UP
  AS IF FOR THE GROUP STAFF MEETING
  NAMED IT A CONFERENCE BECAUSE
  WHY EVER THAT WAS IN MAY
THAT MONDAY, NO MINUTES, NINE
  BOOKS ALL FED NOW TO THE VULTURES,
    GOOD MEMORIES THESE YEARS
       SORT OF
  THANK YOU, WET SATURDAY, ALL
BETS AND PRAYERS OFF – AND JOKES,
      DON'T BOTHER

HUT real, DREAM fleeting, the librarians all
gathered in St Michael's church, altar gone,
rail gone, choir stalls gone, pews gone, there is a
tripping melodic silence. I am at the back and I

ask if anyone knows where I can call a taxi. From
outside I hear a man singing,

One book sing a book,
two book kick a book,
three book burn a book,
four book –

Now I am trying to cross the river in a bathtub
when I am woken
by what sounds like a great wave breaking
over the hut. When I get up to look – it is
three-ninety by the bedside clock – I hear doors
swinging back and forth like waves, must not lose
my spectacles.
Eating my breakfast toast I am
wondering about job satisfaction, and in this mind
I set out for the

Six Book Tea Shack Library Tree House
Annexe

on the cliff path. Up the ladder I can see someone
has left a book. On the window ledge. Tucked
into the book I see there is a note, not good at heights
I am balanced half on a branch now, I reach out

and the book falls. The note says, 'Love me.'
The note as I hold it disintegrates, is dust now.

When I arrive of necessity at Blue Sands Bay the

Four Book

is out floating away elegantly on a
green sea, the librarian waves to me, so I
    sit on the sand and I write this poem:

I hear this note,
outnumbered on the sounding shingle,
defenceless
against claws and nightmares, against
stark whims and inmost fires
catastrophic
    defend me. From
darkest chide
    defend me,
from stinging things and claws,
from human craze,
from mindfulness o'erflown,
especially my own,
not a fun posting, this, no use anticipating
a shared tea break.

Never mind the continuity, must return quickly
to the wood and in the wood
where the librarian, Gwendolyn, new, is cheery,
she tells me Gareth Wyn Evans from upriver
became dizzy with words here once, like
    yesterday.
I say, 'Tell me.'
'Dizzy with words he no longer sings to himself
as he tells he does or remembers he did
cleaning the church once, a once of years.'
'I am the Inspector,' I say, 'I do the rounds, I hear
with my own ears, itch with my own thorns.'
'So?'
'I don't know.'

'Well, bach,' she says, 'just drink your tea, eh?'
I say, 'What Gareth likes best is sorting books,
sorting hymn and prayer books, handing then out
and taking them in again, sorting them.'
'Saying *Amen* as well.'
'Saying *Amen*.'

Now next morning as I tip-toe across the far field
white with light I think of Gwendolyn,
I see in the distance someone pushing, some kind
of barrow, it is not her, I'm sure. Is it?
She is pushing a pram or a table
upside-down on wheels, is it? As I approach
where our paths will cross – now, look, she
pauses – it is not Gwendolyn – saying nothing,
and close by now and I see clearly
in the large pushchair
a steep of books dressed like a baby. She smiles
and it seems easy for her to smile, seems hard.
We continue on now, where *is* she going?
Do I accompany her, at some steps behind if her
                        silence
is professional and my duty is – But I must
smell the sea again, away again so soon at
a weary quickness to the

Three Book

at Blue Sands Bay
                where disguised as myself
I snuggle in
                and I read a little

from Nicholas Saunders,
        'Ecstasy and the dance culture':

'We ended the evening around midnight
with The Doors playing 'The End.''

and from Sue Rowe,
        'Gwen John'
        'Yesterday I came to an old wood – I walked
        on anenomies and primroses.'

It can be done. But it seems one book is out,
these two mint and in need of
fingermarks and soup spills.

Energised I set off uphill and arrive in minutes to

The Man on the Reconstructed Bench

and here he is, older now, holding the bag tight,
is asleep o` snoring and smiling.
I want him to wake and I'll pose him a question.
He does begin to wake and I stay silent and I
move away over the cliff head from where I see
a trip boat – an awkward tide has sloughed it off,
trippers jump out or are helped out, they are
wading in on to the rocks, I want to call down to them
with questions, about survival, about paragraphs.
I hear myself whisper *Lord, we beseech thee,* a leftover,
and find in my pocket yes, milk chocolate
but a wrapper only.

Trusting my new-found energy let's re-visit the

Two Book

where my arrival co-incides with the strengthening
of the full Atlantic storm that explains the trip boat's

sinking. Books on loan with it. But to business, for
through the shaking doorway comes the man
on two sticks and under his arm
      Saint Grotius on Silent Doubt,
and *in lieu* again I become librarian. He glares at me.
I smile at him, I smile indicating patience.
'Doubting utterly at last my own sanity', he offers,
'and sickened beyond belief by the scent of hot scones,
I have resolved to open myself to the gulls, viz, to
slip into sleep on the beach without any dramatic
re-awakening. This menace of a book, date stamp it
out of my life, do me this favour, take your own soul
into care, this blessed book, do not open it. Farewell.'

Job well done, the man well-pleased with himself,
I set out across country to what has been on my list as

Pier Library Rock Point Caff

which muddles me, there is no pier
and no such named rock, no caff either, no library.
There is a caravan. I look in, a robust woman sighs,
      she tells me she is recuperating.
I offer my sincere, fruitful wishes on behalf of the
most senior librarian there is in the universe.
But she spits almost, 'Know your sort.'
'I am,' I whisper, 'the Library Inspector and my
      schedule tells me
there is at this map reference a *vide vacantia* library.'
'How nice for you.'
I say I have from years ago a postcard.
She says, 'It never was a library, it's a caravan *per se.*'
I say *'Per se* is library. It was here, I have a postcard.'
'Never,' she says, 'postcards are pictures.'

'I have a verifiable postcard,' I say again, 'shows

Upper Pier Library

and has scribble, look,
  Having a great read,'
'And it says', she says, snatching it from me,
  Wish you were here, you worm!
In my heart she means bookworm.
I ask if there *are* books.
She says, 'Do you want coffee, my God, or not?!'
I say, 'I sniff shelves, there *were* shelves.'
'Come in and look.' she says, 'and didn't my Gran
stock sugared whelks in them sweet days?'
She shows me in. I say, 'I can smell books.'
'Sugar?' she says.
'Six,' I say, 'O sweetness! O honeyed librarian!'
'Out!' she says.

On such a day chilly out here, freezing.
I confess I saw in a corner and put under my coat,
  Viktoria Tokareva, *The Talisman & Other Tales*:
  'But today everything would be different.'

No great pleasure in being right. Anyway this book
could have been dropped there by mistake in the
possession of the Russian Ambassador on a trip here
glad-handing. Enough for today, must

in the morning trek up
north east of the Bog onwards and upwards far out
north-east of this smallness to the

Library of Pamphlets at Low Top

and here I am, where the librarian, Peggy,
even as I enter asks to see what I am writing.
I say it's a professional secret, will be sent off to HQ.

She says, 'Word gets around, you know, what's said
and what's not said, and jokes, have you heard – look,
the new decor? Do I get good marks for this, Sir?'

So I speak what I have prepared:

> *'What of salvage when the storm has passed?*
> *When the storm has retreated*
> *from the Library of Pamphlets?*
>
> *They flew, soggy still they flew.*
> *They made for the hillside a drapery*
> *and for the clouds a dispersion*
> *of the larger vision. Let us sing ping-pong.'*

'Are you sure you know where you are?' she says,
'Is that what you advise these days?' And,
'Are you sure you've come to where you think
you've come to?'
'Try this,

> *Engine of waves   and of the great winds*
> *and of applauding movement   in earth deep*
> *and deaf to us, to our   special pleadings,*
> *deepening for us with   a few words more*
> *we make our little claim   our fraught claim*
> *as the storms sweep the globe   enabling birth*
>   *to wise worms.'*

'Would tea do as my contribution to this fun?'

Extra-mural, leave it. I must away to spend
a few moments with
the view over the whole coast, to stand and relish
the purposeful glow and flow
in all the libraries under my inspection.

When I send in these deft notes I shall surely
merit – Should have accepted the tea. Even
a biscuit, two maybe.

Believe this if you will, I am here in my hut
with the kettle on, it was late afternoon
on my way home, when a man rose up
out of the river. He was trying to speak.
I was sure he was trying to share something
long remembered. His lips opened and closed,
his face was a rag. A man at all? Then he
sank back into
the still water
just as Wilma Soll appeared out of the little

Bridge Library

that was not there yesterday, looking at me
as if I needed help. I said, 'I hope you keep
a clear and faithful account of fines for books
cheerfully overdue
and for even wise scribbles.'

And I came away, walking quickly and crying
because Wilma's eyes –
and so overtook a man with one hand cut off brutally,
his stare bruised, his wave bloody,
and as I watched him pass, dragging himself along

he waved his one hand at me in a readerly way.
To repeat: In the wood the **One Book Library**
is a shed, in folky chat hospitable to passers-by, I had
hoped so
        as I turned for home.

Another day and I trek back and this time enter the

One Book

where the book, *The Grove, a History* –
can be loaned for a year,
and if the book is out, the caller
is welcome here

for an apology and weed tea
and conversation – seasonal.
Time passes always lightly.

After many years the one book will fracture,
will come away from itself
and however clear the reader's eyes
it will make no sense.

The man with the bloody arm
wanders in singing 'Ring a ring o'roses'
so is given a free weed tea and put first on the list
for when *The Grove, a History*
is in again. He says,
                'I have no story
                nor want for one.'
Not much sleep before rising to make the
long walk along by the sea to the Rock Point

Library of Mystical Visions

is evaporating as Miss Wanderlust comes
floating by and by, once of Regulation Aphorisms
for the whole coast, became too much for her,
redundancy pay did her right proud, she sprites
with the air here, leaps, a big shoal-blue book of tales
falls out of the mirror
                    smashing it.

Days go by, I forget when it was I was last up
the cliff path and no record of it, off again to the

Six Book

SHUT again, new notice:

PERMITS FOR PHOTOGRAPHING
            THE DOLPHINS
FROM THE LIBRARY SITE AVAILABLE
PRICE ONLY £25 A MINUTE PUT
CASH OR CHEQUES THROUGH THE
LETTER BOX. THANK YOU.

I hang about, one man, then another, now
and elderly woman shove cash or a cheque
through the letter box and aim their cameras
at the sea. Rumour has it dolphins are again
out there playing at book tossing.
                    I walk about a bit. From my pocket
my notebook. I write,

    I am sorry really sorry
    I brought no flowers,
    brought no biscuits,
    no apples, no cake,
    I came out of curiosity,

rejoicing in the pitfalls
of my job, I should, yes,
have smiled more. And
growled more. *Bonkers*, I would say
if I were me. Or you.

And posted it through the letter box.
The librarian must return soon in
        professional expectation
of cash and cheques. Good wheeze.

My next note says,
on Bryn Glass Lit Bright in high flurry at the

Ten Book

where sheep have got into the Library,
sheep queueing loudly from across the hillside
to get in, seven queues of sheep are
straggled across the levels. I could join
a queue or I could claim seniority. Begin anyway
as onlooker with the the mystical dialectic of
        hubbub and
brash utility, swim in this snail trail's
        exuberance.
    I write,   'The sheep have it,
        God bless them,
        their lust is word.'

Credit me with moderate staying power,
continue this sad record in the nettle grove at the

One Book

where, covered in bird shit,
the one book lies open
on the door step.

I place the book under an ancient oak,
I collect stray leaves,
I cover the book with these dead leaves.
On top of the leaves
I leave a 10p piece.

And this, on record, a trek to Bog Moor again
to the
Two Book

the door swinging open and again I fill in
as temporary librarian in residence,
sit myself at the table, glaze my eyes.
Here he comes, I don't recognise him,
I have never seen him before
but I know who he is, I know this tale,
that the book heavy in his hand is
Scones in a Day.
He looks fat and sad, I smile.
'Grew my own wheat', he says,
'kept blackberries for sugar
and they lost their sweetness,
stole butter and milk from the farm
at St Mawr's, sour butter, curdled milk,
I became a scones virtuoso.
Is old Calamity Sam the Teeth still around,
has he rushed in lately all smelly aggro?
I should have invited him in for scones –
I am disappointed with myself truly –

an invite annually anyway. Not that I want
     Saint Grotius
but I could have apologised.
We were so young once
and fit for a long life, hell yes.'

What's this? I turn the pages, blanks
many of them, then an entry that
befoggles me:

 '*Causeway Ice Lollies and Cash 4 Poems*

  We buy
  clean and dry poems,
  paired easy to read stanzas,
  neat around and back again poems,
  poems with titles.

  We don't buy
  soiled or wet poems,
  stained poems,
  tattered skiving off work poems,
  ripped poems,
  excessively worn poems,
  poems with the best lines missing.'

Someone was shouting – I am so tired now
writing this in my bed – he was shouting, really,
joyfully – do I mean this? Yes, with joy glowing
or at an end's splut. It was an end, I knew
whose voice it was, that scattered
     and broken voice. I saw the bench
in my gut's eye. This was at Devil's Quay. Elwyn
Emmanuel came running then, stomping anyway,

leaving Tom to graze. Elwyn was
waving a book, he said, 'Floating in the bog, three
of these, by a David someone or other, look. No,
   listen' – held up his finger –
   '*Are roses   red in the dark?*
How about that?!' Broke down, cried, and went,
   the donkey following.

This as I shall note it here now should have been
my undoing at the tideline:

I stand in the rising tide at the Causeway,
something breathes, something
that may be memory.

Mr Caulie stumbles by, who's he?
He says brightly he is Mr Caulie,
he says he's been in charge of
   Central Distribution
until he began to wander away from
Central, said he's happy now because
redundant and making free with the air here,
stumbles like a storm-blown Golem.
   And now, look,

an old book crawls out of the box he has
thrown on to the rock pools,
the box flares out wings and is away
leaving the book to make its own journey.

   The book is sneaking away
              up the beach chased
      by the tide.

I walk
swaying to the tideline, I wait
and I wait and wait, not for anything
especially,
only that to wait
seems right, I wonder
what right would be, dear friends
who may read this when News gets hold of it,
without empathy,
got it sad, I say,
trust me.

Mother said do not laugh until you are sure
of the joke, steady your cheek muscles on
burnt toast, keep a slice or two deep in your

torn coat pockets, make it
easy for yourself, she said, make it hard,
and the

One Book Library burns,

watch it.
The librarian who, to log it now, entertained
me often with punctuation, dandelion tea
and a fig biscuit,
has been taken out,
tortured
and shot
and the library torched, the wood around it

is a fevered ballet of fire, spreading across the river,
which boils,
and the sky is lit red. I have heard screams.

I am collecting rose fragments where in truth there
are nor ever were roses. I am singing this song:

Collecting roses from the beach
                              is hard to bear,
it must be done, every one, every
                              rouge rose here,
if it means petal by petal the whole mile
                              in fear.

They will have no use soon, salty,
                              shrivelled,
the sea will take them, it is good,
                              unregulated,
does take some, brings them back,
                              lied,

now brings them back again or not.
The sea turns white.
The sea was white, now grey, by moonlight.

Collecting and bagging rose petals, yes.

They, the uniformed, them with lust guns,
them in blood lush, in uniform-skins dank.

In lieu of something else I straggle after petals.
O petals taken far out, etcetera, they must
be saved and pressed for leaved love
between the turns of our best books.
Which books are they now? Promised.

Not me, not I, the voice. Exit song, resume duties,
I wobble via the breezy causeway
over smoothed stones to Mog Island, to touch the

Four Book

– gone, has become peripatetic, floated away,
or been hijacked, to nearby Crab Island,
  and there is a black-robed boatman, he
knows me, yes, seems to know me, knows me,
        not that we speak
      as he rows me, nor, his curled
finger to his lips, will he allow thanks, the sun is up
        and threatening
and I am here first, waiting. Surely there would
as ever be
    polite treachery,
    a ganging up against the brainiest,
    pre-planned trickery by way of jest,

    a claimed special relationship with the librarian,
    brazen conceit, but

no need to claim Inspector's privilege, I arrive
and find plenty of nobody. I enter, my schedule says
        should be
Steve Minte in charge here. I sit in his chair.

Congruent – with something or other – a man
on makeshift sticks puts his head around the door –
I suppose he lives here, in the rock pools –
and tries to fix me with his bright old eyes.
        Nothing is said.
This is the last time he will appear, I know it.
He nods his nose and waves a stick. He leaves.
I turn to such busyness as could be helpful here.
        Nothing, but

always I have liked queueing here, must be the slant
of the morning light. It's over, the gulls know it,
I step into the rowing boat and am rowed
to the beach, below the **Three Book,** not on
today's schedule. Need time off anyway, to
check for fire damage. My hut must be OK,
I have slept in it.
　　　　　Need more tea bags, aftermath
of fire outed as hot
　　　　　competes with thirst.

In my pocket some loose pages, with intent to type
and include them in my report, I am not hiding and
I am hiding, chance has rescued me, I shall refuse
to give my name or address, say I am on a mission,
say I love my work. So, in daylight,

Night awakening

And so we become fiction,
from the moment of our birth
we are a living fiction.

There is nothing that we are
that is not subject to subjectivity.

To anyone else we are what they
perceive us to be according to their own
mood, mode and make-believe,

as they are to us a fiction made
by our own for-ever unsettledness.

Night awakening: 2

It eludes surgery, the soul, 'my tunnels
will be for more subterranean than your shafts', Freud
wrote to Jung, *Sing out my soul* is good to sing, the tune
swings it, Max Brod didn't burn Franz Kafka's words,
it's the meadow
        and the small bridge
        over the fresh stream

has the last say perhaps, or it's a person dying alone,
a hut is problematic if it has no balcony
for the night watch, my table is too small to shelter me
during a rain of bombs, no hide and seek,
and of my, *in* my very own soul's camouflage. Bede
        in his
Arts Poetica wrote that the first syllable of *spiritus*
is long, it effects scansion, truth therefore.

Report

Some say the chairs were kicked over
as the librarians left, after the dispute
about the new codes. Or it was air raids.
Others send whispers, that they have never left,
are here hiding in a deep cave, some say
it was wind through the open door
blew the chairs over, others note how one chair
of the same kind stayed upright,
seasonal now, libraries gone almost,
holiday camps everywhere.

Night awakening: 3

I was on the beach playing at Library,
a wave came in right over my head
and it grabbed the sand library and took it
and all the books with it, and I thought but the wave

had brought no books back and it had taken as well
more than were allowed out. The next wave

did bring some of the books back and I said
'Thank you, you can take them again and again
if you want to', and it did, every one of them,

and then the whole sea went far out leaving only
wet, cleaned sand, my lovely sandcastle library was
gone blat,
         for ever.

Plan

Dance a few silly steps on the prom

and refuse coins, arrive at shops

only when closed, at theatres only
at dawn, fold the umbrella only
during rain, kick a ball around
        only on ice.

Night awakening: 4

'Building a poem so that it does not
collapse under the weight of its own importance
nor slip out of shape through scorching sun
or an irregular storm, nor become dulled
         if used wholeheartedly,
nor let its making show like a lazy cook's kitchen
photographed with a shrug. Run along now,
rebuild that tree house library, plant a page,
bury another dead grass snake's eyes, chew hard
on wild garlic and hazel nuts. In the tree house
recite the psalm, *Out of the deep,*
                              until nightfall.

Vitruvius
during the 1st century BCE in Rome – wrote this:

'Bedrooms and libraries ought to have an eastern exposure,
because their purposes require the morning light,
and also books in such libraries will not decay.
In libraries with southern exposures the books are ruined
by worms and dampness, damp winds come up, which
breed and nourish the worms, destroy the books with
mould by speading their damp breath over them.'

Secret holding

Keep books in a coffin on a chest,
juggle *libra* and *liber* to yourselves,
         cold out there,
juggle *liber* and *libra* by the light of

the itching fire,
know by heart that we are free people,
know by gut that we are book people.
    Sing.

Between

Between what remains of the wasteland's libraries
I come of age, suspended in age, vantage clotted.

On the grey slopes and in the gross infertilities
that want, along the dried-up stream dark clouds

drape the dream, wanton blesses vagrancy, skim
whisks breath, here's the donkey with its book bags,

here's the real Inspector whisking his tea with the feather
        of a dead dove
as he surveys sealed mud, to be wrenched by tide
and by tide again and again and again and again
        till gone.

There are voices, they ghost-ride greedily on the
lukewarm wind, songs fall off staves, terse whisper

    stands in for conversation, hey and ho
        wither.

I know where to find the

Secret Book Barn

where at first as I crossed what I thought under snow
    was known land

or might in the distance have been Grace Chapel
    or the old school room
where the land tilted in a voluminous mood swing

that when I crossed over to it saw what it had been,
    when I pushed open
the heavy door, slipping-sliding, hypnotised by the –
                'Stop!'
'Tell no-one', the woman in the heavy wheelchair
    up-eyes me.
I stand cold and hungry on this whole world hill.
    'I have here', she says,
'the only known commentary of St Paul on Plato.'
    I say, 'Show me.'

Men in uniform come kicking the puddles
as they prowl, whacking the grass with guns or with
heavy spades, rehearsing through the wood their
                warps and buckles,
                their teeth
slamming as they go at everything, beheading
bluebells, harebells, any of the lovely bells, planning
we know the beatings, flame-throwers ready now
for when they find books. The whole wood goes up

in forced flames. Never forget this. Under a burned tree
I sit examining what I have written. Made it all up.
Made up none of it. Liar! How dare you!? Easy.

Liability clause

A library is as good as the people who use it,
as wise as the wisdom brought to it,
as trustworthy as its overseers.

This little song I made up as I walked,

as I kicked the track, kicked it harder,
    brusied my head on air

along the track eyes onwards and who is this
wanderer? She is deep inside a purple cloak,
she hugs a red book to herself, visible when the wind
opens the cloak, something is happening
that clears, look, opens and clears vacantly
everything that is. We approach each other
and as we pass she says, 'We spin in space as
        empty of mind
                    as a tide's
wave'. Now

what to do but continue on, my feet pacing
as machine parts on the stony path. And look,

a man in a dark suit is rushing towards the sea
        at Barnacle Bay
waving wildly as if someone is out there dangerously
unaware. I see no-one. I want to see someone,
I want this man's rushing and waving utterly alone
to be worth something.

        He stops where the curls of white trickle in
and he begins to sing some absurd unmelodious clang
of a hymn, his arms out wide, starched, wanton.

He turns abruptly and sees me and I look away.
I look again and he's gone, into the waves.
I turn again, and now rushing down the beach
towards me: Tom,
        the donkey –

Must go now to the school hall on the lane
next-the-bridge over the estuary for the
much hand-to-hand prophesied, whispered,
floated, muttered insider-decreed

PROTEST AGAINST LIBRARY CLOSURES

where I sit at the back, sowester over my forehead,
shopping bag on my lap, please God, someone, no-one
                    directs
any questions at me. No librarians present – or
is that Wilma with Gwendolyn, have those two
been delegated? By whom, though? It begins, a man
leaps up on to the stage and speaks with actorly anger,
listen now,

   'Not that I need any library myself, but I am
   concerned wholeheartedly for my children's future,
   they have books at school, of course, a few
   that I haven't looked at but must be good for them'

and more of that, until interrupted by Jonas Billings,
whom I thought had died in the queue at the

     Ten Book, and he says,

   'I have no money to speak of, I queue
   and am almost always disappointed
   because the bloody library doesn't open

   as advertised, must I stagger across this
   whole terrain on the off chance? And also,..'

There are by my count one hundred and six people
here now from where I can't imagine. There is

shouting and the waving of fists, 'How dare they close
even one of our many wonderful libraries!' – and

the like on and on from voice after voice, 'it's cultural
heresy',

then when Wilma and Gwendolyn get up on the stage
and declare themselves, and take ten minutes to
achieve silence, Wilma speaks:

'How many of you here have used one of our
local libraries these past twelve month?'

Much turning this way and that, nine hands are
raised, one is lowered again, another lowered. On
the way out   I smile
at Wilma and Gwendolyn, they mime scribble and
more scribble and more scribble and they wave and
depart chuckling.

I stand now on the Sacred Hill, the projected site
of the multi-storey
holiday hotel
Quickie Royale

where the **Twelve book** – Hardly matters now how the
fire started, some say in the middle of the night, hardly
matters, or when those foreign troops, or when our own
troops, came, or when I dreamed, or that a book got
torched, or that the land
became tired. And *we* did.

Anselm in Bec to Lanfranc in Canterbury:

'You asked me for the Moralia in Job,

William, Abbot of St Étienne
and Arnost, to be Bishop of Rochester,
have found a scribe,
who has begun to copy our manuscript from Bec.
I am doing my utmost
to get you the Ambrose and the Jerome,
but it is not easy.
There has been a disagreement with the scribe,
we have failed to engage the man
whom you suggested in Brionne,
and no-one who is free to do the work here in Bec
is sufficiently competant.'

I wake at dawn
and I walk out around my hut, look, past the river, look,
where the church was, where it has gone, humming
is coming from the grassy mound, and on the mound
            the librarians. They are
            breathing free, they are
gathered, the air hums. One of them sees me,

now they all see me. They are throwing books
at me, heavy books, a storm of books is coming

and I want to list them, need more time. Seems
I am moving on
            to a new posting, and here already
outside my burned-out hut is Elwyn and his donkey Tom
to take me
            to where the Hooded Vultures
            are hungry.

Meanwhile the monk far out at the sea's edge has moved, is very wet, must be. He is shaking the sea off himself, into the bright sunset. Easy to see the greater wave breaking over him, blotting out the sun. There was still time and the work had to be done.

Notes and Acknowledgements

Short excerpts on page 29 originate from the following: W R Dawson, *The Huxley papers: A Descriptive Catalogue of the Correspondence of Thomas Henry Huxley.* Ludwig Wittgenstein, *Tractatus Logico-Philosophicus.* Virginia Woolf, *The Waves.* Iris Murdoch, from *The Sea, The Sea.* A E Housman, *A Shropshire Lad*, Poem XXVII. *The Eclogues & Georgics of Virgil* translated by T.F.Royds

Page 41: '*As the astronomers tell us....*': Charles Dickens at the Birmingham and Midland Institute, September 1869, in 'Speeches by Charles Dickens', 1881.

Page 80 : *Vitruvius:* Original as prose, trans. Morris Hicky Morgan, USA, 1914/1960.

Page 85: *Anselm in Bec to Lanfranc in Canterbury*: A poem made from prose. From 'Lanfranc of Bec' by Margaret Gibson, 1978. I bought it in 2000 sold off by the then Central Library for 40p.